OLD-TIME
FARMHOUSE COOKING

BY

BARBARA SWELL

Photo Courtesy of Mars Hill College, N.C.

"The homes of a nation are its strongest forts."
Farm Journal magazine, 1882

ISBN 1-883206-41-3   Order No. NGB-37
Library of Congress Control Number: 2003104284
© 2003 by Native Ground Music, Inc.
Asheville, North Carolina

INTRODUCTION

Can you stay for dinner? This old farmhouse kitchen's a mess; I've been up cooking since dawn. We're not having anything fancy, just that cranberry pot roast simmering on the back of the wood cookstove, along with some sweet corn and red ripe tomatoes from the garden. I just took this oatmeal bread out of the oven and we have fresh-churned butter and blueberry jelly to go on top. Now, my husband just loves his pie, so I made a blackberry and an apple. That rukus you hear out on the back porch is the kids churning vanilla custard. What good's a pie without homemade ice cream, anyway? Grab a chair and let's eat.

While this farmhouse feast sure sounds tasty, we all know that farming has forever been frought with hard times and never-ending work. But still, we cling to the romantic notion that the country life is a better life. Having lived both in the country and the city, I say, give me a hoe and home-grown food any day! Fortunately, with the increasingly abundant roadside stands and farm markets of today, you can live a city life and still find farm fresh ingredients for the delicious comfort-food dishes of days gone-by.

The recipes included in this book were collected from a wide variety of American agricultural journals published between the 1880's and the 1950's. In an attempt to preserve the folklore of hand-me-down cooking, you will find that all of the recipes are written in their original form. Because old-time farm wives were skilled cooks and didn't need to measure, the directions are vague and can be difficult to interpret by today's cooks. That's why you'll find an "author's note" following most of the recipes. I also couldn't resist offering an alternative to the saturated fat-laden dishes enjoyed by so many hard working farm families of decades past.

Whether you're a born farmer or a country-minded city person, I hope you'll enjoy these creative rural American dishes, with an added dash of popular culture, from a time when the food was wholesome and life was full of fresh air and sunshine.

CONTENTS

"The housewife makes the home, and the home makes the nation."
The Housewife magazine, 1891

THE FARM KITCHEN

Food always tastes better cooked on a wood cookstove. I've heard it said a hundred times, and it's true. Maybe beef stew tastes better slow-simmered on the back of the stove for hours and biscuits are more fun when they're a little browner on the side that was closest to the firebox. Or maybe, you're just plain hungry because you've been splitting wood to fuel the fire. But I think food always tastes better when you're not in a hurry making it, and if you cook with wood, you take your time. So if you want to simplify your life, cooking with wood is a great place to start. Let's get you a stove.

Photo Courtesy of the Library of Congress

WILL YOU MARRY ME?

Buying a wood cookstove is like buying a car, choosing a pet, and maybe even finding your spouse all rolled into one. You'll be happiest if you give lots of thought to your decision first! Whether you buy new or vintage, simple or fancy, bringing a cookstove into your life is a commitment. Well, unlike your spouse and your pet, you can always bail out and use your stove for furniture, but you won't regret finding the right match to start with.

> *"The range is the most important thing about the whole house, and you cannot afford to risk anything because it is cheap; a poor stove or range is expensive at any price."*
> *The Majestic Range Cook Book, 1890*

THE FARM KITCHEN

THE VINTAGE COOKSTOVE

Take my advice: do your research and start out with the right stove! These gems can weigh 500 lbs. or more, and are a nightmare to move. Vintage cookstoves, if used every day from the time they're new, will last about 25 years before important parts start wearing out. Don't be taken in by appearances. They can look great,

The author feeds her 1928 Home Comfort cookstove.

but might not be at all functional. When considering a stove, bring a flashlight with you and inspect every inch of it, inside and out. The firebox grate is the first part to go, and warps and cracks in the cast iron in any part of the stove are a bad sign. Setting your stove up correctly once you get it home is as crucial as choosing the right one to start with.

WOOD

Fire up your cookstove. It's time to dance. You'll feel like a choreographer as you open and close dampers and drafts to control the heat and move your pans around in search of just the right spot on the cooktop. But nothing's as important for cooking as the wood you put in the firebox in order to get the fire you want.

Pine and poplar make good kindling, but you'll need to add some hardwood to sustain the fire. Maple, cherry, and ash burn long, but oak's hotter. For even, hot oven baking, I favor black locust, apple, or hickory. Of course, you'll love the appetite you'll work up from all the chopping you get to do, because cookstove wood needs to be about two inches square, and that's pretty darn small. (See page 70 for more information on cooking with wood.)

THE FARM KITCHEN

THE ICEBOX

"The household ice refrigerator is the final link in the chain by which food gets from the farm producer to the family table in the most wholesome condition possible. The health and welfare of the civilized world leans heavily upon the ice industry and its success. Failure of all the ice plants in the United States would spell serious danger of a plague."　　　　　　*Iced Dainties, 1928*

T hrilled by the promise of glamour and more leisure time, American housewives of the mid-1930's were quite pleased with their new electric refrigerators. However, no such pleasures were available to electricity-deprived 1930's rural farm wives. Northern farmers were still storing blocks of sawdust covered pond ice in ice houses to be used in summer months while the southern farm refrigerator was most often a springbox.

In 1930, only 13% of farm homes had electricity. With the passing of president Franklin D. Roosevelt's 1936 Rural Electrification Act, that number jumped to a whopping 33% by 1940. The ambitious project was daunting and called for a change of farm lifestyle, so many farmers had to be convinced of the merits of electricity. This poem was part of the "Get Electricity to Your Farm" campaign:

Electricity is a servant, make it work for you.
Then baking days won't be so hot, or washdays be so blue.
Your cows will be contented, with a milker fine and bright;
The kids will like the music, from the radio at night.
Your feed will be ground easily, your baby chicks kept warm.
The whole family will be happy, with electricity on the farm.
　　　　　　　　　　　　　　　　　　　Author Unknown

SOUPS AND STEWS

GEORGIA GUMBO
Home Demonstration Club Cookbook, 1950

4 slices bacon
2 cups fresh tomatoes
2 cups okra, chopped
Salt and pepper to taste

1 large onion, chopped
2 cups fresh cut corn
1 Tbs. sugar

Fry bacon in a heavy frying pan and remove most of fat. Cook onion in the pan until light brown. Add rest of the ingredients and cook until thick enough to serve with a fork.

FRESH TOMATO SOUP
Rural New-Yorker August, 1926

One peck (one-fourth bushel) ripe tomatoes, one bunch celery, seven onions, three green peppers, 14 bay leaves, 14 whole cloves, 14 sprigs parsley, 1½ cups flour, ½ lb. butter, 3 Tbs. salt. Put the tomatoes, celery, onions, and peppers through the meat chopper. Tie the bay leaves and cloves in a muslin bag. Mince the parsley. Combine these ingredients and heat to the boiling point. Blend the flour, butter, and salt and add to the mixture. Pour into sterilized jars and process for one-half hour. This amount will make about five quarts. To serve, heat and dilute with the desired amount of hot milk.

Author's Note: Follow current USDA guidelines for canning safely. This freezes well in canning jars or plastic freezer bags. I GUESS you could use canned tomatoes, including juice, omitting salt.

SOUPS AND STEWS

Photo Courtesy of Alice Lloyd College, Ky.

MRS. HILL'S IRISH BEEF STEW

¾ lb. stew beef, cubed
Salt, pepper, flour
1 onion sliced
2 carrots, diced

2 diced potatoes
1 Tbs. chopped parsley
2 Tbs. oil

Sprinkle the meat with salt, pepper, and flour and brown it with the onion in the oil. Add water to cover. Cover pan and cook slowly until meat is almost done, about 1½ hours. Add potatoes and carrots and cook until tender, about 25 minutes. Add parsley. Makes 4 servings.

A Knight's Advice

Better to die with harness on, in smoke and heat of battle,
Than wander and browse, and fall anon, in quiet of meadow-
land cattle.
Better to gain, by arm or brain, chaplet of laurel or myrtle,
Than bask in the sun, with work undone, and live one's life like
a turtle.   Successful Farming *March, 1915*

HARVEST BREADS
~

BUTTERMILK BISCUITS

*Biscuit making is an art. The best thing you can do is to find some-
one who makes the biscuits you love and have them show you
how they do it. The flour's the most important ingredient. Here in
the south, White Lily is a hit. But my favorite flour comes from
The Old Mill of Guilford in Greensboro, N.C. (336-643-4783).
Whichever flour you choose, make sure it's fresh soft spring wheat,
which is low in gluten, for tender flaky biscuits.*

2 cups self-rising flour   About ¾ cup buttermilk
¼ tsp. baking soda   6 Tbs. butter or shortening

Mix flour and soda. Cut in butter or
shortening. Make a well in the middle
and add enough buttermilk to get a soft
dough you can work. Turn out onto a
floured board. Knead the dough a few
times until it holds together well. Roll
out ½ inch thick and cut with biscuit
cutter or a glass dipped in flour. Cut
straight down without twisting or the biscuits won't rise well. Place
on a well-greased cookie sheet and bake in a preheated 450⁰ oven
12-14 minutes until they're browned just the way you like.

To Make Biscuits Light
Farm and Fireside, 1907

- *To make biscuits light, drench with gasoline and ignite before
  serving.*
- *Quickest way to get rid of peddlers, buy all they have.*
- *How to remove fruit stains from linens, use scissors.*
- *To keep the children at home, lock up all their clothes.*
- *To keep hubby at home, lock up his toupee.*
- *To economize on coal, get a gas range.*
- *To test the freshness of eggs, drop them on some hard surface.*
- *To propitiate (appease) the cook, it can't be done.*

9

HARVEST BREADS

CANDIED GINGER CORNBREAD

Definitely not southern cornbread. (They eat theirs crumbly and NOT sweet.) This moist, hearty, sweet bread is great for breakfast with eggs, bacon, and grits! Make the effort to get stone-ground cornmeal, if you can find it. As any cornbread snob will tell you, you must bake this bread in a well-seasoned cast iron skillet!

1½ cups self-rising cornmeal	6 Tbs. melted butter
½ cup self-rising flour	1½ cups milk
½ cup candied ginger, minced	1 egg
¼ cup sugar	

Timing is everything for good cornbread. Read through all these instructions before you begin. Heat the oven to 450°. When hot, put your cast iron skillet in to warm up. Meanwhile, mix the dry ingredients and ginger. In another bowl, whisk the milk, and egg. Now, pull out your skillet, stick your butter in there and put it back in the oven. Add your wet ingredients to the dry and stir a few strokes; pull your skillet out of the oven and add most of the butter to your batter, stir a few more strokes. Pour the batter into your hot skillet. Bake about 25 minutes or until golden brown.
Author's Note: No self-rising meal or flour? Just add 2 tsp. baking powder and 1 tsp. salt to the dry ingredients.

CORNMEAL CRISPS
Home Demonstration Club Cookbook, 1951

Sift together 1 cup cornmeal, ½ cup flour, ½ tsp. salt, ¼ tsp. soda. Add 1/3 cup milk and 2 Tbs. melted butter. If more milk is needed, add 1 tsp. at a time. Knead about 10 minutes. Break off pieces of dough the size of a quarter and roll thin on a floured board. Bake on ungreased baking sheet in a 350° oven. Brush with melted butter and sprinkle with salt while hot. Makes two dozen. Good served with soup our salad. A nice variation is to sprinkle with cheese before baking or chili powder after baking.

HARVEST BREADS

BOSTON BROWN BREAD
Successful Farming February, 1915

Technically a "pudding," simmer this bread on the back of your cookstove on a blustery winter day as you cook the rest of your supper and do some kitchen chores. Graham flour is whole wheat.

1 cup graham flour	1 tsp. salt
1 cup cornmeal	1 tsp. soda
1 cup rye flour	1 tsp. baking powder
2 cups buttermilk	1 cup molasses
1 cup raisins	

Stir the flour and meal into the milk. Dissolve the soda in a little warm water and add it to the mixture along with the remaining ingredients. Stir all well and turn into a greased bread mould. Cover tightly, and steam three hours. When done, turn out and bake in oven five minutes. A tin lard pail with smooth sides and tight cover makes a good mould.

Author's Note: This recipe will make two loaves. It's easily halved. Mix the dry and wet ingredients separately. Add wet to dry along with raisins and stir just until combined. Bake in a buttered 13 oz. coffee can covered tightly with foil and secured with a large rubber band. Cut a couple of vent holes in the foil. To steam, place the can in a sauce pan with boiling water that comes halfway up the can. Keep pan covered and simmering, adding water as needed. Steam about 2 hours, then test with toothpick to see if it's done. The raisins will sink somewhat, but that's part of the fun!

HARVEST BREADS

SWEDISH ORANGE-RYE BREAD
Farm Journal and Farmer's Wife January, 1940

Also called Kaka-brod, this bread is both hearty and fragrant. Rye flour makes a sticky dough. Resist the temptation to keep adding flour while kneading, or your bread will be dry.

2 cups hot water	¼ cup brown sugar
1 package yeast	5 Tbs. melted butter
1½ cups rye flour	2 tsp. salt
3 Tbs. molasses	3-4 cups white bread flour
Grated rind and juice of one orange	

Pour hot water over rye flour, salt, sugar and molasses. Stir until smooth and cool to lukewarm. Sprinkle yeast over mixture and stir in well. Add butter, orange rind and juice. If you have the time, you can let this mixture "work" for about 5 hours for a very light textured bread. Add white flour gradually, keeping dough soft. Knead 5-10 minutes until you become a sticky mess. Put the dough in a greased bowl and let rise until doubled. If you let your dough "work" earlier, this will take 20 minutes. Otherwise it will be at least an hour. Divide dough into 3 pieces, stretch out round to ½ inch thickness on greased cookie sheet or parchment paper. Let rise until doubled. Prick with a fork and bake in a 375° oven until browned.

To keep cured pork during warm weather, it should be wrapped in parchment paper or old newspaper, then enclosed in heavy muslin or canvas and covered with ordinary lime whitewash to which has been added a little glue. Hang in a cool, dry cellar.

Successful Farming, 1915

HARVEST BREADS

NO-KNEAD OATMEAL BREAD
Home Demonstration Club Cookbook, 1951

1 cup oats   ½ cup molasses
2 cups milk   2½ tsp. salt
1 Tbs. melted butter   4½ cups sifted flour
1 pkg. yeast dissolved in ½ cup warm water
1 cup raisins (optional, but highly recommended)

Pour hot milk over oats and let stand until lukewarm. Add yeast, molasses, salt, butter, and half the flour; beat well. Stir in remaining flour; cover and allow to rise in warm place. When light, pour into greased bread pans and let rise again until doubled. Bake in a hot 425° oven for 15 minutes, then reduce heat to 350° and continue baking for 35 minutes until lightly browned.

The Mill in the Woods.   *Photo Courtesy of the NC Archives and History*

HARVEST BREADS

VERNA'S ICEBOX BUTTER BUNS
Farm Journal and Farmer's Wife May, 1940

Straight from the 1940 Farmer's Wife's "Country Woman's Cupboard," these no-knead crescent rolls are easy to make. Just throw them together the night before, and roll them out the next day.

1 pkg. yeast	1 egg, beaten
2 Tbs. warm water	2 tsp. salt
¼ cup sugar	½ cup melted butter
2 cups warm milk	5-6 cups sifted flour

Combine yeast, water, and sugar. When dissolved, add milk, egg, salt, then two cups of the flour. Mix, add melted butter, and enough additional flour to make a smooth dough. Do not knead. Cover, let stand in icebox overnight to get stiff enough to handle. About three hours before rolls are needed, divide dough into thirds. Flour your bread board and roll each piece into a large thin round. Cut into 12 pie-shaped wedges. Roll up each piece from the outside toward center into a crescent. Place on a greased pan. Do not crowd. Allow to stand 2 hours, or until doubled in size. Bake 12-15 minutes in a preheated 425° oven until lightly browned.

Find the weak spots in your fences and yourself, then strengthen them.

Pin your hopes on your own crop.
                    Farm and Fireside
                    September, 1907

HARVEST BREADS

HOT CROSS BUNS
Farm Journal & Farmer's Wife April, 1940

I tweaked this recipe just a tad by omitting cloves and adding lemon rind. If you don't like citron, substitute dried, sweetened pineapple and feel free to increase the amounts of dried fruit.

1 cup milk	3½ cups sifted flour
¼ cup sugar	1 tsp. salt
2 Tbs. butter	1 tsp. cinnamon
1 pkg. yeast	¼ cup chopped citron
¼ cup warm water	¼ cup raisins
1 egg, beaten	Rind of ½ lemon

Scald milk, add sugar and butter and cool to lukewarm. Dissolve yeast in warm water, then add egg and warm milk mixture. Stir well. Add all remaining ingredients to make a soft dough. Knead until smooth (15 minutes), let rise 2 hours. Make into about 15 balls and place on a greased cookie sheet. Let rise until nearly doubled in bulk. Cut a cross with a sharp knife lightly on each and bake in a preheated 375° oven for about 20 minutes until lightly browned.

Frosting:
¾ cup confectioners sugar
3 Tbs. softened butter
Lemon juice

Beat sugar and butter. Add lemon juice and continue beating until you get a stiff icing. Using a pastry bag (or a plastic baggie with a trimmed tip), pipe a cross over each warm bun.

Farm Wives Save Two Ways, 1927
"Try this for the next two weeks: Let every other loaf of bread you bake be raisin bread. Note how your men take to raisin bread. Note that they eat more bread and less of the more expensive foods. You'll save more expensive foods and save leftover bread."

HARVEST BREADS

BALTIMORE APPLE BREAD
Farm and Fireside February, 1907

The author of this recipe intended for you to fill this fragrant bread with applesauce made from late-ripening tart apples such as Wealthy, Blenheim Pippins, or Snow apples (also called Fameuse or Chimney). These now old-timey varieties are still available because they taste so darn good. Seek them out whenever you get the chance! Homemade apple butter makes a good filling, too.

"Rub through a pound of sifted and warmed bread flour, 2/3 cupsful of butter and 3 heaping teaspoons of sugar. Dissolve a cake of yeast in a cupful of milk that has been scalded and cooled to lukewarm. Add to the flour and mix to a stiff batter. Add 3 eggs well beaten, and beat the batter until it blisters. Cover and let rise overnight in a warm place. In the morning, it should be doubled in bulk. Divide into two portions and roll out in cakes ½ inch thick. Spread one with rather tart well-sweetened applesauce, cover with the other and let them rise together about half an hour. Bake in a moderate oven until well done. As soon as taken from the oven, spread with more applesauce and dredge lightly with sugar. Sprinkle with nutmeg or cinnamon and set back in the oven long enough for the sugar to melt. Eat very hot."

Adapted recipe: Make as above, but with the ingredients below. You could kill yourself beating this batter with a spoon until it blisters, so add enough flour to make a soft dough and turn onto a floured board. Beat the dough with a rolling pin about 15 minutes, lightly dusting with flour, as needed, to keep from sticking. Bake bread at 375°, about 15 minutes. I prefer to skip the last applesaucing and instead brush the bread with melted butter, then sprinkle with cinnamon sugar when you pull it out of the oven.

3-4 cups flour	1 pkg. yeast
½ cup butter	¼ cup sugar
1 tsp. salt	1 egg
1 cup milk	

DAIRY & EGGS

I f a farm woman of 1907 needed some petty cash for her own pleasure or a splurge for her family, she'd raid her stash of egg and butter money. If she needed to support herself and her children, poultry and dairy cows often provided the means to do so. Here's one Texas widow's story:

200 Eggs a Year Per Hen.

How to Get Them.

"I will tell you how I make a living for myself and three children. Last year, I kept 35 nice Plymouth Rock pullets and 3 roosters; sold $30 worth of eggs, $20 worth of frying-size roosters, keeping 100 hens for hatching this year. Next, I bought one bronze gobbler and two turkey hens. From them I raised 25 young turks. I milked two cows and sold 170 pounds of butter. In the summer, I cooked for my brother-in-law's harvest hands for a few weeks, and every spare minute, I would run out and pick cotton from the cotton patch near my house. I think there is more money in poultry and cows, for a woman on a farm, than anything else when they are managed right."

Farm & Fireside August, 1907

Balked
Farm & Fireside February, 1907

Old Farmer: "No, I don't want any more of your labor-saving machines. I've tried enough of 'em. Look in there. There's a typewritin' machine the missus spent all her egg and butter money on to get fore me, 'cause I ain't so over-handy with the pen. Just look at the swindle."
Friend: "What's the matter with it?"
Old Farmer: "Matter! Why you can't even write yer name with the bloomin' thing unless ye know how to play the pianner."

DAIRY & EGGS

Photo Courtesy Library of Congress

THE POULTRY QUEEN OF IOWA
Farm and Fireside, 1907

"Mrs. Johnson, of Iowa, was a woman of too much spirit to waste any time in vain repining when she found herself with a husband suddenly incapacitated, and four little children looking to her for their support. She decided that there was money in eggs and chickens, and she set to work to demonstrate some of her theories. Mrs. Johnson took a thermometer and made a record of the temperature at which her laying hen, Madame Biddy, kept her eggs. Then she constructed an incubator of her own, using a couple of old wooden boxes. In this homemade contraption, she put one hundred and sixteen eggs, and kept her lamps burning carefully for three weeks. One hundred and five little chicks later, Mrs. Johnson would go into the chicken business and she would make it pay. She has succeeded so well that she is now known throughout the West as the "Poultry Queen of Iowa."

"In eight years, Mrs. Johnson made a living for the family, paid the help, bought farm machinery, built a new house, barn, double cribs, hog house, poultry house, smoke house, ice house, wash house, and three brooders, and paid a debt of $14,000 on her mortgaged farm. She says, "I have two sons in college, and old Biddy is footing the bills.""

DAIRY & EGGS

TOMATO SURPRISE
Farm and Fireside July, 1907

Maybe you want to be surprised, and maybe you don't. You can really only pull this one off with fresh, sun-ripened tomatoes.

Select round tomatoes of even size, peel, and when firm from being thoroughly chilled, cut in two and remove the centers. Break carefully into each half a fresh uncooked egg, dust with salt and pepper. Cover with a layer of thick white sauce, then one of grated cheese. Cook in a hot oven until the egg is set.

Authors Note: Don't half the tomato, just core and remove center. If you have some "thick white sauce" sitting around, use it. Otherwise, just top with cheese and bake at 400° until egg is set.

Photo Courtesy of the Library of Congress

DAIRY & EGGS

WELSH RAREBIT
Majestic Range Wood Cookstove Cook Book, 1890

Call it rarebit or rabbit, this English tavern fare has enjoyed popularity in America since the 1700's. By the end of the 19th century, this simple and versatile dish was served off the cookstoves of the farmer and from china chafing dishes of the wealthy for breakfast, dinner, or supper. Over time, rarebit evolved into the bland and boring melted processed cheese mess we remember from the 1950's. Forget those days and make it with a strong ale and good aged cheddar cheese over thick slabs of hearty homemade whole wheat bread or serve it over lightly steamed broccoli.

One and one-half pounds of fresh cheese, one tablespoon of fresh butter, one tablespoon of dry mustard, one-half pint of beer. Put butter in chafing dish. When nearly melted add cheese in small pieces, mustard next, and a little paprica (sic). Add a small amount of beer to prevent burning, and keep on adding beer until all is used. Serve on toast.

Photo Courtesy of Mars Hill College, N.C.

Author's Note: Have all ingredients at room temperature. Melt a tablespoon of butter in a double boiler. Add gradually 1½ cups grated sharp cheese, then 1 tsp. dry mustard, a dash paprika, and a little cayenne pepper. Whisk until melted. Add beer bit by bit until you get the consistency you like. Pour immediately onto thick slices of toasted whole wheat bread and broil in oven until top begins to brown.

DAIRY & EGGS

Way Back When
New England Farm Life June, 1929

To the Editor: "Way back in the eighties, when I was a farm boy on the plains of Kansas, I used to carry a pail of golden butter six miles to the old country store and exchange it for groceries for the family. Back over the hills barefooted I'd go, the hot dusty road burning my blistered bare feet. Sometimes I got a nickle's worth of red stick candy that seemed a gift I would not forget. Those were the days when it didn't take money to make people happy. We just grew our happiness as we went along."

From the Editor: "Great days those were neighbor, sure enough. Fifty years hence, another crop of old codgers will be telling of a lightning-swift aeroplane age, what joys they had away back in '29 creeping around in motor cars."

Dairyisms
Farm Life September, 1927

"Now," said the teacher, "what bright little boy can tell me five things that contain milk?" "I can!" shrieked a freckled-faced youngster, "butter an' cheese an' ice cream an' two cows."

Lady to Jimmy the new milk distributer: "You say this milk is pastuerized?"
Jimmy: "I'm sure it must be lady, all our cows are turned out to pasture."

DISHES FARM MEN LIKE

B y the time 1940 rolled around, farm women were enjoying a social life outside the farm. Electricity had reached a third of American farms, bringing with it conveniences such as electric refrigerators, ranges, washing machines, and vacuum cleaners. Women had more time to socialize and exchange modern recipes for new, lighter foods that would supplement the usual farm fare they were tired of preparing day in and day out. Evidently, their husbands were not happy. The March, 1940 edition of *Farm Journal and Farmer's Wife* magazine gave a voice to miserable farm husbands forced to eat fluffy, fancy foods that were "all the rage" at the time. Don't you feel so sorry for them?

DEAR WIVES OF WRONGED HUSBANDS

"Big strong farmers have been crying their hearts out on my editorial shoulder for so long, pleading for hot biscuits, homemade bread, and he-man breakfasts. When we asked the men to tell us just what IS wrong with their wives meals, farmers said:

'We're tired of fussed-up concoctions. We want hearty, homey foods like steaks, roasts, succulent cooked vegetables, savory stews and meat pies, potatoes with good gravy, sizeable lettuce salads or slaw, corn bread, hot cakes and country sausage or ham and eggs, and strong, hot coffee.'

And Pie! How these men hunger for good flaky, crusted pie. None of these meringued, chiffony things, mind you, but first class apple, pumpkin, custard, or cherry pie."

DISHES FARM MEN LIKE

Photo Courtesy Library of Congress

TO THE WIVES: HOW DO YOU SCORE?
(Based on the most frequently voiced complaints)
Farm Journal & Farmer's Wife March, 1940

1. Have you had a real steak or roast dinner this week?
2. Was todays a farmer's breakfast, quite a bit more than fruit juice, toast, and coffee?
3. Do you avoid asking him "What shall we have for supper?"
4. Do you have a list of his favorite foods and do you prepare them frequently?
5. Have you variety in your meals without using your husband as a human guinea pig?
6. Do you plan meals ahead, not just last minute frying-pan, can-opener, bakery meals?
7. Do you reserve fancy fixings for women guests?
8. Do you receive compliments on the excellence of your pot roast, meat pie, biscuits, corn bread, apple pie, gingerbread, and other so-called old-fashioned foods?
9. Was today's dinner on time? Hot things hot?
10. Can your plain cooking pass without need of garnish, because it is well cooked and seasoned and nicely served?

DISHES FARM MEN LIKE

FARM HUSBANDS WHINE
Farm Journal & Farmer's Wife March, 1940

Dear Foods Editor:

Food is to eat. Woman can have their pretty salads, but give me food that'll stick to my ribs. Farming's hard work and I have to keep up my energy. I want meat every day and I don't care how many dieticians tell me I don't need it. I like savory pot roasts, fresh homemade bread, a big pot of baked beans and brown bread, Indian pudding, and pies. Give me steak, french fried potatoes and apple pie, and I positively purr.

Dear Foods Editor:

My wife is a culinary dresser-upper, a show-off. I'm the guinea pig on whom she tries out pineapple marshmallow whipped cream salads. Sometimes, I think she adds a dash of perfume. I want potatoes browned with pot roast, thick pea soup with a chaser of johnnycake, chicken pie, beefsteak with hashed browned potatoes, roasted spare ribs and sauerkraut, a seaworthy Irish stew. Someday I'm going to chain my wife to the stove leg and have them all!

Dishes Farm Men Like

I'm Agin' the Vitamin
Farm Journal & Farmer's Wife March, 1940

I've eaten Vitamin A and B,
I'm about fed up with Vitamin C.
Each day I cram down Vitamin D,
And also a lot of Vitamin E.
Now if there's Vitamin F and G,
I've et 'em all, clear up to T.

Now I want to be right up-to-date,
And I want to keep the proper weight.
But all these vitamins get my goat,
Some day I'll grab my hat and coat.
And hunt up a good hamburger stand,
That hasn't any vitamin brand.

You'll think I'm rather a funny dub,
But I like good old-fashioned grub.
I wish my wife would cook some ham,
And make hot biscuits with plenty of jam.
Or a good hot bowl of chili soup,
For fancy salads, I don't give a whoop.

My granddad is a hale old man,
But grandma wasn't a vitamin fan.
And he ate lots of pie and cake,
And all the good things they used to make.
My wife's a good cook, I won't complain,
But I like good food and I like it plain.

DISHES FARM MEN LIKE

FRIED CORNMEAL MUSH

This is really polenta. If you want to get your 1940's farm husband riled up, add garlic, oregano, and sun-dried tomatoes.

2 cups cornmeal	2 cups cold water
1 tsp. salt	1 qt. boiling water

Mix cornmeal, salt, and cold water. Add slowly to boiling water, stirring constantly. When thick, cook slowly on the back of the cookstove, 1½ hours. Pour in a bread pan, first rinsed in cold water. Smooth top, cool until firm. Slice ½ inch thick, brown on both sides on a hot skillet in a little fat. Serve with maple syrup.

Author's Note: In case you don't have a wood cookstove, try making it in a crockpot. Butter the sides of the crockpot and add 6 cups boiling water to the salt, cornmeal, and any other seasonings. Cook on low 6-9 hours and continue as above.

COOKING FOR MEN
Rural New-Yorker November, 1926

"Here are a few things I have learned about cooking for men. They like plain well-cooked food best, not so many kinds at one meal, but plenty of each. For breakfast, the cooked cereals, eggs, bacon and hash, also fried cornmeal mush with syrup, griddle cakes with sausage and syrup are all good. Potatoes with meat of some kind and a vegetable make the foundation for dinner, along with hot breads made from cornmeal or whole wheat flour. Men like pie for dessert. Molasses cake with lots of raisins is easy to prepare and delicious.

Most women like to make something different once in awhile, but men are apt to pass along dishes that they are not familiar with."   -Mrs. R.G.

DISHES FARM MEN LIKE

H ere's a little test for you. If you can decipher and bake this hearty bread (that farm men like), then you win the prize! It comes from my collection of beloved yellowed, food-spattered recipe cards. I'm guessing it's from the 1920's. Here it is exactly as typed:

GR.NUT BREAD "BRIGHAM"

2 C.Sifted Graham Flour.
I C.Flour, I C.Br.Sugar, I T,S.
I T,B.P. I t.Soda, I C.Nuts.
2 C.Sour Milk, I Hr.350

HE-MAN MEAT AND VEGETABLE SOUP
Farm Journal & Farmer's Wife March, 1940

This is part of "a satisfying supper" that also includes crackers, rolls, and hot gingerbread with whipped cream.

1 lb. soupbone	3 stalks celery, sliced
1 cup dried lima beans	2 potatoes, diced
1 large carrot, diced	1 onion, sliced
1 large turnip, diced	2 cups chopped cabbage
1 can corn	1 pint whole tomatoes
1 bay leaf	Salt and pepper to taste

Put lima beans to soak. Wash soupbone, cover with cold water. Cook slowly 3 hours, adding seasonings and lima beans the last half hour. Remove bone, skim off fat. Reheat to boiling. Add vegetables, except cabbage and corn. Cook ½ hour, add corn and cabbage and cook 15 minutes more. Remove bay leaf, add meat pieces from bone and serve very hot.

NERVY WOMEN

I f you think that most early 20th century American farm women lived a life of servitude, at the beck-and-call of their demanding farm husbands, then read these stories. Early agricultural magazines, which were intended to be read by both men and women, as well as vintage personal diaries were full of accounts of women who were just fine running the farm on their own, thank-you. Mary Atkeson asserts in her classic 1924 book, *The Woman on the Farm,* that "in the big and important business of farm and home, the farmer and his wife are equal partners."

A COUNTRY GIRL'S ADVANTAGES
by Kittie Turner
Farm and Fireside August 25, 1907

"There seems to be any number of misguided people on this old world of ours who in some unaccountable way have possessed themselves of the idea that when a country girl is grown she has just two alternatives ... to get married, or go to town for employment, that there is no way in which she can be independent and yet remain in her farm home. For the disillusionment of those individuals, I want to tell how I not only supply my own needs, but have a nice little sum at interest in my own name."

Okay, so it turns out Kittie Turner was a teenager who possessed the energy and drive of 82 normal people, combined. Here's her story: She's tending her abundance of old-fashioned flowers one summer when a hotel keeper walks up and asks her if she would sell him bouquets on Saturdays for his Sunday tables. At 5 cents per arrangement, Kittie does well for a girl in 1907, but why stop there? She figures other hotels and restaurants may want the same. Sure enough they do, and the money's piling up. What the heck, why not sell her customers fresh-ground horseradish from her garden, too. It was taking over anyway.

NERVY WOMEN

Then comes the pillow industry. While going "chokecherrying" and "graping" with her mother one fall day, Kittie gathers a bag of wild hops, which was at that time, a popular remedy for various miseries including sleeplessness. Of course, now everyone wants a hop pillow to sleep on. Business is booming, especially when Kittie's swamp-gathered cattail pillows and even softer milkweed pillows are added to the line. But no pillow sells as well as the $2.50 balsam needle pillow, which nets a hefty $2.48 profit each.

"After the busy horseradish-grinding and flower-planting days of spring, the bouquets of summer and fall, the pillow industry-not only of autumn, but of nearly all the year, there are yet several months of idleness during the winter," says Kittie. *"Then it is that I get my best licks at Old King Corn."* You guessed it. She's gone into the hominy business. With hotels, restaurants, grocers, and neighbors clamoring for the hominy, she can't keep up with the demand. Oh, well, the customers will have to do without, because Kitty's in school and has her home duties to attend to as well.

"Now I haven't told you all my ways of earning money in my country home. I'm afraid if I did there would be too great an exodus among the girl readers of the towns. My mother says I help her more than nine tenths of the girls do, and my father thinks I will be an old maid. But however that may be, I know I will never have to marry a man just for the sake of a home and support."

"And I just want to say in parting, girls, that if all of you would make up your minds to be independent, to make the most of every little opportunity that presented itself to that end, there would not be one tenth the unhappy marriages there are when the question of support takes precedence over congeniality and real love."

You're already behind. In the time it took you to read this story, you could've canned 12 quarts of pickles, and stitched three quilts!

NERVY WOMEN

WOMEN FARMERS TO THE RESCUE
Farm and Fireside October, 1906

"One woman who lives on a little farm in Lake County Ill., does all the work of her farm. Dressed in a gingham skirt that reaches the top of a pair of high-laced course shoes, and with her head in sun bonnet, she plowed the land for five acres of oats, five of corn, and a ten acre fruit and vegetable patch. She did all her own cultivating, cut fifteen acres of Timothy grass with a mowing machine, raked it, loaded it, and hauled it to her barn. She cares for and milks eleven head of cow, and takes care of a variety of poultry. She lives alone and attends to all her own housework. Rising at five, she works all day, rain or shine, reads her papers after supper, and retires at nine. Now she is 55-years-old and doesn't look a day over two score. She is probably the happiest woman in Lake County. It has been the work of these such nervy and muscular women that rich crops this year have been saved."

Photo courtesy of the NC Archives and History

MEATS

Vintage American agricultural magazines didn't print many meat or poultry recipes for their readers. Most housewives boiled, baked, roasted, or fried their meat for dinner and then consulted recipes to make use of those pesky organs or leftovers. How about these 1927 farm magazine dishes: Sliced beef tongue, chicken loaf, veal timbales, fried brains and eggs, and kidney stew. I don't know about you, but none of these dishes appeal to me, so I've included in this chapter, the more traditional comfort-food meat dishes that have warmed farmer's innards for the last 100 years.

MEAT LOAF
Farm Journal and Farmer's Wife
November, 1940

Climb down off your tractor and kick off your work boots! It's meatloaf for dinner . . . with mashed potatoes and gravy, buttered carrots, whole wheat rolls and a peach pie for dessert.

1½ lbs. ground beef	1 cup milk
½ lb. lean sausage	1 egg
½ onion, chopped	Sprinkle of sage
½ cup bread or cracker crumbs	

Mix all ingredients thoroughly. Shape as a loaf in a large open pan. Bake 1½ hours in a moderate 350° oven until meat is cooked through.

Q: Why is a planted potato like a door post?
A: Because it will propagate.
Successful Farming, 1915

MEATS

MAPLE BARBEQUE GLAZED PORK BALLS
From a 1940's recipe card.

1 lb. lean ground pork	¼ cup chopped onion
½ tsp. salt	1 egg, beaten
2 Tbs. water	¾ cup bread crumbs
2 Tbs. parsley or other fresh herbs, chopped	

Mix the above ingredients well, and roll into balls the size of a walnut. Place in baking dish. Pour glaze over all and cover with foil. Bake at 350° for 20 minutes. Uncover and bake about 15 minutes more or until glaze thickens. Serve over hot rice.

Glaze: Combine 1/3 cup barbeque sauce, 3 Tbs. maple syrup, and ½ cup water.

CRANBERRY POT ROAST
From a 1940's handwritten recipe card.

3 lb. beef chuck roast	2 cups fresh cranberries
2 Tbs. fat (olive oil)	1 cup water
2 Tbs. flour	Salt and pepper
	1 orange

Coat roast with flour, salt and pepper, and sear in olive oil until browned on all sides. Cook the berries in one cup boiling water, just until skins pop. Then add berries and cooking water to meat along with the orange, cut into about 8 pieces. Simmer on low in a covered Dutch oven, about 3 hours, adding water as needed.

Author's Note: Add 1 cup red wine or broth (beef or chicken) to the cooking liquid in addition to the cranberry water.

MEATS

PILGRIM PIE

Rural New-Yorker November, 1905

Definitely not a recipe for beginners, this pork pie is authentic and tasty. Why, it was a 1905 farm husband's idea of a good time. Oysters, a Victorian era fad-food, bullied their way into an amazing array of meat dishes, such as this one. Feel free to omit them in this recipe.

Cut a two pound piece of fresh pork into dice, after it is cooked, and prepare the following crust:

1 pint mashed potatoes	1 tsp. salt
1 Tbs. butter	¼ tsp. pepper
¼ cup milk	1 tsp. baking powder

Enough flour to make a crust, which can be easily rolled out one inch thick.

Put alternate layers in a baking-dish of the diced pork, raw oysters, minced parsley, a light dusting of summer savory, finely shredded onion with salt and pepper to suit, and one tablespoonful butter. Cover with a brown sauce. Fit a cover of the potato biscuit and bake in hot oven 20 minutes. Five minutes before it is finished, draw out, cover with fine cracker crumbs mixed with one egg. Return to the oven to finish browning; garnish with parsley. This potato crust is excellent for any meat pie.

Author's Note (to those of you who already know how to cook): Season and bake a pork roast. Drain off most of the fat, then make a clear gravy from the drippings, adding some wine, water, and enough corn starch to thicken. Serve the roast one night, and make the following dish with the leftovers: Place slices of pork in a large baking dish or skillet, top with a little diced onion, sprinkle with summer savory, salt and pepper to taste, then cover with the gravy you made. Put the potato biscuit on top and bake at 400° until the biscuit is lightly browned and the gravy bubbles.

MEATS

MRS. TWEED'S BAKED HAM & YAMS
Good Victuals From the Mountains, 1951

Take a 2 inch thick slice of ham, put it in lukewarm water that covers the ham and let it stand 40 minutes. Drain. Place in deep baking dish, cover with pineapple juice and thick slices of peeled, raw sweet potato. Put lid on baking dish and bake in a moderate (350°) oven 50 minutes. Remove lid. Sprinkle 3 Tbs. of brown sugar over potatoes and add 1 Tbs. of butter. Continue cooking 15 or 20 minutes. Spoon baking gravy over potatoes before serving.

LITTLE MEAT PIES
Farm and Fireside, 1907

There's No Excuse for Dirty Milk!

Are you one of those people who uses cookbooks for ideas rather than recipes? Well, this one's for you. These meat pies are supposed to be cooked in a gem tin, a cast iron or tin pan, sectioned into eight to twelve little rectangles for small whole wheat breads, muffins, or little meat pies. While gem pans are no longer manufactured to my knowledge, you can still find some wonderful ones in excellent shape where antiques are sold.

"Make pie crust and mold in gem tins. Make meat stew chopped fine and seasoned well. Fill the molds and bake moderately fast for twenty minutes. Bits of roasts or ham can be used in this way."

Farmer Mack: "Gee but you're bowlegged. A hog could run through your knees, couldn't it?"
Farmer Jones: "Well, I'll stand still while you stoop down and test out your theory."   *Farm Life* November, 1927

THE POULTRY HOUSE

NC Archives and History

Chicken House Blues
New England Farm Life June, 1929

*I hate the darned old chicken house
From floor boards up to ceiling;
I do not think it's haunted
But it gives me a creepy feeling.*

TURKEY ROLY-POLY
Rural New-Yorker January, 1927

*This is a good dish to make with
Thanksgiving leftovers. The recipe
suggests you steam it like a pudding
for one hour, but most of us wouldn't
do that. Baking works just fine.*

Make a biscuit dough and roll ½ inch thick into a rectangular shape. Spread with finely chopped turkey, moistened with a little gravy, then top with salt and pepper. Roll up like a jelly roll. Bake in a hot (400°) oven 25 minutes or until biscuit is cooked through.

Chicken Sayin's

- *She's as cocky as a bantam rooster.*
- *It's like a bug arguing with a chicken.*
- *It's as warm as a chicken in a basket of wool.*
- *It's a sad barnyard where the hen crows louder than the cock.*
- *When bugs give a party, they never ask the chicken.*

THE POULTRY HOUSE

CHICKEN PIE

What could be better than a golden, flaky-crusted, hot chicken pie after a long day's work on the farm? But the chicken pies we think of today, with chunks of chicken and vegetables in a thick creamy sauce were not what you'd be eating 100 years ago. If you bit into one of these pies in 1900, you'd end up with chicken bones in your mouth and you'd gain about 4 pounds. Here's a typical chicken pie recipe from Farm and Fireside, 1907:

"Cut two chickens into small pieces as for fricassee; cover the bottom of the pie dish with layers of veal and ham placed alternately; season with chopped mushrooms and parsley, pepper and salt, then add a little gravy. Next, place in the dish the pieces of chicken in neat order. Now fill all cavities with slices of hard-boiled eggs; repeat the seasoning and the sauce, lay a few thin slices of dressed ham on the top; cover the top with strips of puff paste. Egg the pie over with a paste brush, and bake it one hour and thirty minutes."

CHICKEN POT PIE
Home Comfort Cookstove Cook Book, 1933

Here's an old-timey recipe that won't surprise your mouth with bones or give you a heart attack. It's actually chicken and dumplings. If you want to make a crusted chicken pie with vegetables, see page 39.

Stew a cut chicken (or chicken breasts) slowly until tender. Boil broth down until it just covers the chicken. (Bone the chicken at this point.) Season broth to taste with salt and pepper. Drop tablespoonfuls of dumpling dough onto broth and chicken, cover, and cook undisturbed for about 15 minutes.

Drop dumplings: Sift together 2 cups flour, 3 tsp. baking powder, and ½ tsp. salt. Rub in 2 Tbs. butter. Mix ½ cup milk with 1 egg and add to dry ingredients. Add more milk until you get a soft dough (that's too soft to roll out).

VEGETABLES

A nybody who farms, gardens, or frequents local produce stands knows that the vegetables that ripen at the same time are the ones that taste best together. For guaranteed success, try different combinations of the following:

Spring: Beets and greens, scallions, spinach, lettuce, peas, cabbage, broccoli, baby carrots, cabbage

Mid Summer: Squash, onions, cucumbers, bush beans, early tomatoes, peppers

Late Summer: Pole beans, tomatoes, onion, corn, eggplant, potatoes, lima beans, okra, carrots

Fall: Turnips, kale, winter squash, pumpkin, rutabagas, spinach and other greens. Don't forget to add fall apples, nuts, and sausage (pigs were slaughtered in the fall).

CARROTS WITH BEETS
Farm & Fireside August, 1907

A great example of eating same-seasoned vegetables together, this dish is quite colorful, as well as healthy. Cook the vegetables separately, substitute a splash of balsamic or rice vinegar (for the 2 Tbs. vinegar) and add a squirt of honey along with the butter.

Put one cupful of diced boiled carrots and two cupfuls of diced boiled beets into a stew pan with two tablespoonfuls each of vinegar and butter. Season with salt and pepper. Let get very hot, and serve.

OLIVE AND NUT STUFFED CELERY
Farm Life November, 1927

Carefully wash and dry very crisp celery. Mix cream cheese with finely chopped walnuts and minced pimento stuffed olives. Fill celery stalks with the mixture.

VEGETABLES

STUFFED SAVORY SWEET POTATOES
Farm Life November, 1927

Here's a creative sweet potato dish. If you prefer sweet over savory, add ¼ cup brown sugar, a sprinkle of cinnamon and substitute fresh orange juice for the milk. These look great on a platter.

3 large sweet potatoes	¼ cup milk
1 egg white, beaten	¼ cup pecan meats
1 Tbs. butter	Dash salt and pepper

Bake sweet potatoes and when done, split in half, lengthwise. Scoop out the potato and put into a bowl. Add the milk, butter, (and sugar if you like), and beat for thirty seconds. Then fold in egg white, seasoning, and nuts. Refill the shells and place one or two marshmallows on top. Bake in 350° oven about 15 more minutes.

Those Savage Boys
Farm Journal August, 1882

"Here we have a girl's composition on boys*: Boys are very stubborn; you have to use the potato-masher to make them mind. They never will clean their boots on entering the house. Boys are the fag-end of humanity; they will lay awake half the night inventing mischief. Every cook needs a boy in the kitchen to eat the hard pie and bread-crust. Little boys are the cause of the few old maids in the world, they drove away the beaus. Boys are fast becoming savages; they chew and smoke, drink all kinds of intoxicating drinks and swear. Mr. Editor, if you think it worth the ink-let the boys have it!"*   -Farmer's Daughter

VEGETABLES

VEGETABLE PIE, PEANUT BUTTER CRUST
From a 1940's handwritten recipe card.

You just have to give credit to whoever created this recipe. It probably came about because the family was low on shortening and a container of peanut butter was sitting on the shelf along with last summer's canned vegetables. The recipe makes enough for a large, hungry farm family. You can easily halve it.

3 Tbs. butter	16 small onions
5 Tbs. flour	1 cup cooked peas
1 tsp. salt	1 cup lima or string beans
½ tsp. celery salt	3 carrots sliced ½ in. thick
3 cups whole milk	

Make sauce, add vegetables and cover with crust.

Crust:

1½ cup flour	4 Tbs. peanut butter
3 tsp. baking powder	½ cup milk
1 tsp. salt	4 strips raw bacon

Roll crust to fit pan. Cut bacon very fine and sprinkle over top. Bake 20 minutes at 425° until bacon is crisp and brown.

Author's Note: Make sauce from ingredients in the top left column. Melt butter in frying pan and stir in flour. Cook on low heat, stirring constantly until paste begins to brown slightly. Add milk, a small amount at a time, whisking until smooth. Cook until thickened and THEN add salt to taste (this recipe is too salty). Pepper is good, too. Cook your vegetables lightly and add to sauce. Make the crust as you would biscuits (see page 9), then sprinkle raw bacon on top and bake as above.

VEGETABLE CHICKEN PIE

Make the above recipe, substituting chicken broth for half the milk. If you use canned broth, omit salt. Add as much cooked chicken as you like along with the vegetables. Feel free to substitute butter or solid shortening for the peanut butter in the crust recipe.

CORN

C orn has always been a big deal to the American farmer. Appearing as animal feed, cornmeal, hominy, syrup, and moonshine, it has long been a winning crop and a cultural icon. Oh, but nothing's as good as tender summer sweet corn, just pulled from the stalk. Smell the earthy green husk and bite into the cobb right there in the garden . . . that would be right after you flick off the worm from the end of the cobb. The best tender corn loses its sugar quickly, so you want to cook it within hours (or minutes) of picking.

TOMATO & CORN CASSEROLE
From a 1930's handwritten cookbook journal.

4 large tomatoes, sliced	2 cups corn, cut off cobb
2 small, diced onions	Salt and pepper
½ green pepper, diced	½ cup bread crumbs
¼ cup grated parmesan cheese	

Place vegetables in layers in a well greased casserole. Salt and pepper to taste. Crumble 2 slices of bread and lightly brown in a pan with 2 Tbs. butter. Toss crumbs with parmesan cheese and sprinkle over vegetables. Cover pan lightly with foil and bake in a preheated 350° oven 20 minutes. Remove foil and bake 10 minutes more.

National Corn-Husking Meet

Modern mothers know that sweets should be included often in the lunchbox, because sugar is turned at once into energy. Why, just the other day, at the National Corn-Husking Meet, the champion ate brown sugar 20 minutes before entering the contest. And he won! Rural New-Yorker *February, 1936*

125,000 people turned out for the 1940 National Corn Husking Contest held in Davenport, Iowa. It's said that "the contestants held a celebrity status much like the professional athletes of today." National Corn Huskers Hall of Fame

CORN

GREEN CORN PUFFS

This recipe comes out of an early 20th century handwritten cook-book. The New England farm wife who wrote this journal got her corn right off the cobb, of course. Store-bought sweet corn won't work well in this recipe; it's too tough. You'll either have to grow your own, or buy it from someone who does. To grate corn, cut the kernals off, then scrape the remaining pulp off the cobb.

Two eggs beaten light	1 pint grated corn
1 cup milk	Dash red pepper
Grated cheddar cheese	½ tsp. salt

Combine eggs, milk, corn, salt and red pepper. Fill small dishes 2/3 full of above ingredients and top with soft grated cheese. Steam or bake.
Author's Note: Pour batter into well-buttered muffin tins or custard cups. Bake in a preheated 400° oven until set.

Champion Speller Cultivates Corn, 1927

Photo Courtesy of Ferrum College

"Dean Lucas, a 13-year-old-boy won the National Spelling Contest by spelling "abrogate" properly. Here he is cultivating corn on his father's farm just after his return as champion speller. This boy lives on a 200 acre farm and most of his training for this spelling contest was done while doing farm chores and trapping fur-bearing animals. The elder Lucas seems to be a back-to-the-lander, a motorman who left town to run a farm because he thought the open country the best place to raise a family. Dean Lucas won $1,000 as a prize for his spelling."

TOMATOES, TOMATOES

T here's something sacred about a home-grown tomato; even though they take over your life from August until November. You may hear us weary tomato-sauce-canners complaining briefly, but you sure won't see us eating a store-bought hard and tasteless winter tomato. Nope, we shamelessly stuff ourselves with our delicious little darlings for three months and only eat what we have managed to "put up" the rest of the year. These recipes come from *The Rural New-Yorker*, 1926. Notice how desperate Ethel has become by October trying to use up her tomatoes in cookies!

POINSETTIA SALAD
Rural New-Yorker August, 1926

Remove the skin from tomatoes. Divide each tomato into five sections, leaving them slightly connected at the bottom. The sections will then fall apart at the top, giving the appearance of a Poinsettia flower. Take equal parts of chopped celery and nuts and moisten with mayonnaise. Take a tablespoon of this mixture and place in the center of the "flower." Serve on lettuce leaves.

DEVILED TOMATOES
Rural New-Yorker August, 1926

Put two tablespoons butter in a frying-pan and add one-half teaspoon onion juice (or chopped onion), one-half of a tablespoon dry mustard, a pinch of red pepper, one tablespoon sugar, one teaspoon salt (use ½), and one tablespoon vinegar. When the sauce is smooth and hot, lay in four of five medium size tomatoes cut in half, and cook until the tomatoes are tender.

To peel easily, drop cored tomatoes into boiling water for 30 seconds. The skins will slip right off. To quickly seed, give peeled tomatoes a squeeze, most of the seeds will squirt out.

TOMATOES, TOMATOES

ETHEL'S NICE TOMATO COOKIES
Rural New-Yorker October, 1926

I taste-tested this recipe on 15 friends and family and not one of them guessed this was a tomato cookie. I mean, if someone handed you a filled sugar cookie, would you guess "tomato, right?" I don't think so. My taste-tester's minds told them they were eating a fig, raisin, or date-filled cookie. Only when I told them it was tomato, did they say, "cool" or "gross, how could you?" It's well worth the trouble it takes to make these surprisingly tasty cookies, if only to watch your friend's reactions.

Sugar Cookie:

¾ cup salted butter	1 tsp. vanilla
1 cup sugar	1 tsp. baking powder
1 egg	2½ cups flour

Cream softened butter and sugar. Add egg and vanilla and beat until fluffy. Mix baking powder with flour and add to other ingredients. Beat until blended. Chill until dough is firm. Form chilled dough into a ball and knead a few times until smooth. Divide into four sections. Refrigerate two. Roll other two out into same sized rectangles (onto floured waxed paper) about ¼ inch thick. Spread half of the tomato filling on one rectangle, topping with the other. Repeat with remainder of dough. Flip the dough onto a greased baking sheet and bake at 350° until lightly browned, about 20-25 minutes. Cut into squares when cooled.

Tomato Filling:

Combine ½ cup each of unsalted tomato sauce, brown sugar, and raisins. Add the juice of ½ lemon, and a pinch of salt. Cook on low heat 30 minutes until thick, stirring constantly toward the end. Cool and lightly chop in food processor.

The more we sit down at our work, the faster we get it done.

Farm Life September, 1927

APPLES

Apples just love maple syrup. Here are a few recipes from the Janary, 1927 issue of *Rural New Yorker* that will make good use of those apples getting soft in your cellar.

APPLE DOWDY

Line a dish with a thick layer of cooking apples, cover with biscuit dough, bake until done. Serve bottom side up, with cream and sugar, or maple syrup. This is improved by sprinkling the apples with a pinch of salt, a few "dots" of butter, and a little cinnamon or nutmeg, whichever is liked.

Author's Note: Toss 4 cups of peeled and sliced cooking apples with ¼ cup brown sugar, ¼ cup maple syrup, a tablespoon of butter, a teaspoon of cinnamon, and a tablespoon of flour. Place in a skillet or baking dish, wrap tightly with foil, and bake about 20 minutes at 350°. Make a recipe of biscuit dough (pg. 9), and roll it out the same size as your baking dish. Remove foil and place dough on top of the hot apples. Turn the heat up to 425° and bake about 10-15 minutes more until biscuit is browned and cooked through. Invert onto a platter and serve right away.

MAPLE APPLES

Pare and core tart apples. Fill centers with maple syrup, cover and bake at 350° about 40 minutes, or until tender. Serve cold ornamented with pyramids of whipped cream.

PORK STUFFED APPLES

Remove cores from blossom end of apples and fill with a mixture of chopped cooked pork, raisins, and bread crumbs, moistened with maple syrup. Cover and bake as above until apples are tender.

APPLES

FARMER'S APPLE CAKE
Home Demonstration Club Cookbook, 1951

This unique caramalized apple cake "wows" everyone who tries it. See note below for an easier, but still delicious version.

Three cups dried apples washed, cut in small pieces and soaked overnight in just enough water to cover. Next morning put 1 cup of molasses in a saucepan on the stove and bring to a boil. Add chopped apples with liquid; let simmer two hours, cool and add to cake made as follows:

½ cup butter	1 Tbs. soda
1 cup sugar	½ tsp. salt
2 eggs	½ tsp. nutmeg
2 cups flour	1 tsp. cinnamon
Buttermilk	1 tsp. ginger (optional)

Cream butter and sugar; add the eggs and beat thoroughly. Sift dry ingredients and add alternately with the molasses water and milk. Stir in apples. Bake in a well greased cake pan in a moderate (350°) oven. Serve warm with vanilla ice cream or whipped cream.

Author's Note: You can use four to five cups fresh firm apples instead of dry. Add ¼ cup water and 1 cup molasses to sliced apples and simmer on lowest heat for at least an hour. Pour cooled cooking liquid into a measuring cup and add buttermilk or milk until you have one cup. Continue following the above directions. You can add walnuts and/or rum-soaked raisins to the batter for a special treat.

"Jimmy," called his mother. "Who gave you that apple?"
"Sylvia Brown," he promptly answered.
"And what did you say to her?" she asked.
"I told her to shut up her crying."   *Farm Life* June 1929

PIES

No-Fear Pie Crust

"Don't be scared. It is just pie crust." So says Aunt Chick, queen of pies, inventor of the Crispy Crust pie pan, and author of the 1938 book called "Aunt Chick's Pies." Here's her recipe for a 2-crust pie with abbreviated instructions. It takes practice to make a great pie pastry. Keep trying, and if you can, find a pie queen to teach you in person.

  2 cups flour*   1/3 cup butter
  3/4 tsp. salt   1/3 cup solid shortening
  5 Tbs. ice water

Mix flour, salt, butter, and shortening with pastry cutter or two knives until mixture resembles coarse crumbs, or small peas. Add water a spoonful at a time until you can form dough into a ball. Divide in half, wrap in waxed paper (remember this was 1938, use plastic wrap), and refrigerate 30 minutes. When chilled, roll dough out on a lightly floured board into 12 inch circles from the center out. Don't press hard. Place in your pie pan. The top crust can be a solid piece or you can cut it into strips for a lattice-topped pie.
*Use a light spring wheat biscuit flour (not self-rising) or pastry flour for the tenderest crust.

Deep Dish Apple Orange Pie
Farm Journal and Farmer's Wife January, 1941

  1½ quart sliced tart apples ½ cup raisins
  2 tsp. grated orange rind   1 Tbs. butter
  ½-¾ cup sugar   Flaky pastry crust

Put apples in a fairly deep baking dish, sprinkle with sugar, raisins, and grated rind. Dot with butter, and add a tablespoon or two of water. Cover with pastry rolled thicker than for ordinary pie. Bake 15 minutes at 450°, reduce heat to 400° for 30 minutes.

PIES

HUCKLEBERRY PIE
Rural New-Yorker July, 1926

This is a simple recipe, all except the huckleberry part. Huckle-berries are little wild blueberries that grow in high mountains and ripen in mid-to-late August. Their flavor is intense and the experience of picking them is even better. If you've ever spent a whole day picking enough berries for just one pie, I don't need to tell you that these berries deserve your most perfect pie crust! No huckleberries? Well, blueberries will work, just add an extra tea-spoon of corn starch and please, use fresh ones!

2½ cups huckleberries	1 Tbs. cornstarch or flour
½ cup sugar	Pie crust (top and bottom)

Line the pie plate with the pastry, fill with the huckleberries, dredged with corn starch. Sprinkle with the sugar and a pinch of salt. Moisten the rim of the lower crust with cold water and place the upper crust on top. Be sure to perforate the upper crust so that the steam may escape. Pinch the edges of the two crusts together and flute. Bake 30-45 minutes in a moderate (350°) oven until filling bubbles and top is lightly browned. Keep an eye on it!

Soggy Crust?
To keep the upper crust of fresh fruit pies from sinking into the juice and becoming soggy, use ½ tsp. baking powder in the flour when mixing. This will raise the upper crust just enough out of the juice and you will find it dry and crisp when ready to serve.

The Progressive Farmer January, 1900

PIES

THE SECRET LANGUAGE OF PIE
Rural New-Yorker, June 1927

Wouldn't it be nice if fruit pies grew on trees? The colorful language used by the woman who wrote this column makes you wonder if she didn't grow pies right there on her farm. Unfortunately, it turns out that "pie timber" is a 19th century term for pie filling and "pieplant" is rhubarb. Oh, well, this 1927 excerpt certainly paints a colorful picture of a busy mid-June farmhouse kitchen.

"I have just put the last 'berry pie timber' pie in the oven, and it reminded me to make a note that I didn't can enough of this the past year. I thought it might help some other farmer's busy wife if I told her about these good pies, and she could be prepared for next winter. In between mowing and raking, and caring for little turkeys and chickens, I sprinkle some sugar over my fresh-picked berries. Then when I get a little time I cut up about as much pieplant as there are berries. I put a little water on this, cook until tender, sweeten to taste, then put in the berries and cook a few minutes,

 and can hot. This method works well when the 'good man' comes rushing in to say 'How soon can you go and mow?' Off the stove go the berries to wait until I come in to get a meal, for we can do pie timber when it isn't hay weather. Or perhaps a little turkey has had an accident and must be cared for, but this canning will keep, and it is so good in the winter."

He: "If we get married, I wonder if you can make pies like mother used to make?"
She: "And I'm wondering if you can make money like father used to make!"   Farm Journal December, 1921

PIES

CREAM RASPBERRY PIE
Rural New-Yorker, August 1926

You won't believe this recipe. It's a removable-crust pie; what a great idea. The suggested cream filling is not good . . . an insult to fresh summer raspberries. Fill the cooled pie with softened vanilla or chocolate ice cream instead, and freeze until serving time.

Line a pie plate with a rich pastry; fill with sweetened raspberries, cover with an upper crust but do not pinch down. When cooked, cool the pie, then lift the top crust and pour upon the fruit the following mixture: One cup whole milk, one tablespoon granulated sugar, one-half tablespoon cornstarch, made smooth with a little of the cold milk, and the whites of two eggs beaten stiff. Scald the milk, add cornstarch and sugar and cook three minutes (until thickened.) Add egg whites and chill. Pour into the pie and set aside to chill.

A Pie Proposal, 1926

Who says Rural New-Yorker *is not a good advertising medium? The young woman who made those cherry pies described on page 827, received an offer of marriage "sight unseen." She will continue to make pies at the same old stand.*

DESSERTS

LEMON SNAPS
Country Gentleman, 1902

As with most recipes from 1902, this one's vague. These cookies are just too good to pass up, so look below for an adapted version.

Cream together one-half cup of butter and one cup of sugar, two eggs, beaten light, one teaspoonful of lemon extract or juice, one-fourth teaspoonful of soda dissolved on one teaspoonful of sweet milk, and flour to make a stiff dough. Roll very thin, cut with fancy cookie-cutter and bake.

Adapted Recipe:

1 cup sugar	½ tsp. soda
¾ cup butter	3 cups flour
2 eggs	1 lemon, juice and grated rind

Photo Courtesy of Mars Hill College, N.C.

Cream butter and sugar; add eggs and beat until fluffy. Add soda and mix. Add the lemon rind and juice, reserving 2 Tbs. juice for later. Blend in flour, one cup at a time. Form into two rolls, wrap in waxed paper and freeze. When firm (an hour or two), slice thinly, and place on a buttered baking sheet. Brush tops with reserved lemon juice and sprinkle lightly with coarse sugar. Bake in a preheated 350° oven 8-10 minutes or until lightly browned. Don't leave the kitchen! They brown quickly.

Says the doctor to his patient's wife: "I don't like the looks of your husband." "Neither do I," the wife replied, "but he's good to his children."   The Furrow, 1938

DESSERTS

COCONUT CARAMEL MERINGUE CHEWS
Farm Journal and Farmer's Wife February, 1941

Amaze your friends at the next quilting party with these moist, delicious, very unique cookie bars. To keep the meringue looking good, they're best served the day they're baked.

½ cup butter	1½ cups sifted flour
¾ cup sugar	1 tsp. baking powder
2 eggs, separated	½ tsp. salt
1 tsp. vanilla	½ cup brown sugar
½ cup sweetened coconut	

Cream butter, add white sugar, egg yolks (I use only one), and vanilla. Beat until light and fluffy. Add flour sifted with baking powder and salt. Mix well and press into the bottom of a square baking pan. Beat whites until stiff, beat in brown sugar, then coconut. Spread meringue on top of dough and sprinkle with more coconut. Bake 30 minutes in a moderate (350°) oven or until lightly browned. Cool, cut into squares.

Photo Courtesy of the NC Archives and History

DESSERTS

SOUTHERN FIG AND PECAN COOKIES
Home Demonstration Club Cookbook, 1951

¾ cup butter
1½ cups brown sugar
1 egg
¼ milk
1 cup dried figs, cut fine
1 cup chopped pecans

3 cups flour
½ tsp. cinnamon
½ tsp. salt
2 tsp. baking powder
1 tsp. vanilla

Cream butter and brown sugar. Beat in egg and milk. Sift dry ingredients and blend well with creamed mixture. Stir in figs and nuts. Form into rolls and wrap in waxed paper. Chill until firm. Cut thin slices and bake on well greased cookie sheets at 375° about 12 minutes. Makes 6 dozen cookies.

MRS. BEAMAN'S GINGER SNAPS
The Farmer's Wife December, 1909

1 cup molasses, 1 cup brown sugar, 1 cup shortening, part butter, part lard. Stir and put into a basin and heat; when heated, stir in one tablespoon soda, 1 heaping teaspoon each of ginger and cinnamon, 2 eggs beat light, flour to make a dough just stiff enough to roll out.

Author's Note: Melt 2 sticks butter (forget the lard), stir in 1 cup each of molasses and brown sugar. Mix in 1½ tsp. soda, 2 tsp. ginger, 1 tsp. cinnamon, 2 eggs, 1 tsp. vanilla. Add 3 cups flour, one cup at a time. Chill until dough is firm. Knead dough on a floured board, sprinkling on additional flour, until it's stiff enough to roll out. Refrigerate half and roll the other half out ¼ inch thick. Cut into desired shapes and bake in a preheated 350° oven about 10 minutes or until done.

DESSERTS

THANKSGIVING FRUIT CAKE
Rural New-Yorker November, 1905

My grandmother, Maudie Smith, used to make her fruit cakes at Thanksgiving, wrap them in rum-soaked cheesecloth, then we'd eat them for Christmas. They'll keep this way for months, you just have to store them in air-tight tins and re-rum the cheesecloth when it dries out. Read through this whole recipe first, and assemble your ingredients before you start mixing. You can substitute dried pineapple or apricots for the citron if you like.

2 cups flour	¾ cup currants
1 Tbs. cocoa powder	¾ cup raisins
1 tsp. cinnamon	½ cup diced citron
¼ tsp. nutmeg & cloves	½ cup diced dried figs
1 tsp. baking soda	

Sift together the dry ingredients and combine half of it with the dried fruit. Cream together ½ cup butter and 1 cup brown sugar. Then add in successive order, according to the usual method of mixing butter cakes, the yolks of two eggs, the grated rind of a lemon, half a cupful of molasses, half a cupful of milk, the flour mixture, the fruit mixture and the stiffly beaten whites of two eggs. (Pour batter into a greased and floured tube pan.) Bake in a moderate (325°) oven for about an hour, until cake is firm.

Making apple butter in a copper pot, 1909.

Photo Courtesy of NC Archives and History

DESSERTS

THREE PLAIN DUTY CAKES
Country Gentleman October, 1902

"To supplement the handsome loaf and the layer cake, there is in some families a constant demand for cakes convenient for plainer usefulness. These tried receipts (recipes) are offered as helps, they are for the boys and for every day service."

Give me a plain cake any day. The currant cards and seed cakes are actually soft cookies that would keep well, if not so popular. Bake the cream cake in mini loaf-pans or a fluted cakepan.

CURRANT CARDS, 1902

Soft and chewy, you just can't stop eating these delicious cookies.

½ cupful of butter
½ cupful of sugar
½ cupful of good molasses

1 egg
2 tablespoons sour cream
1 tsp. ginger (use 2 tsp.)

1 scant teaspoon of soda dissolved in a tablespoonful of hot water
2 tablespoonsful of Zante currants (use ½ cup currants)

Stir in flour to make a dough as soft as can be handled. Take it out on a well-floured board and roll to a quarter of an inch in thickness. Cut in oblongs about 2 by 3 inches. Bake in a hot oven to a rich brown. If successfully made, these little cards will be both light and melting in texture and very appetizing.

Author's Note: Cream butter and sugar, add molasses, then egg, sour cream, ginger, soda water and blend well. Add about 2½ cups flour, chill dough until firm, and add up to ½ cup flour in order to be able to roll out the dough. Bake at 350° about 10 minutes.

DESSERTS

SEED CAKE, 1902

One half cupful of butter, one cupful of sugar, two eggs, one half cupful of cold water, three cupfuls of flour, two teaspoonfuls of baking powder, a saltspoonful* of salt and two teaspoonfuls of caraway seeds. Knead, roll out to a quarter of an inch in thickness, score the top in cross lines and sprinkle with coarse granulated sugar. Then cut as in the preceding, or bake in sheets, as preferred. Both these and the currant cards keep well in a closed jar.
* That's antique saltspoon (use 1/2 tsp. salt.)

GRANDMOTHER'S CREAM CAKE, 1902

This is actually a nutmeggy loaf cake. You can substitute 2 teaspoons of vanilla for the nutmeg, if you prefer. If you don't have a cream-pail or milk-pan, use full fat sour cream.

This very old-fashioned cake, once very popular, is as good as it was in grandmother's day (1850's), and worth reviving. It used to be made with a soft, light brown sugar, now difficult or impossible to obtain. Two-thirds of a cupful of butter, two cupfuls of sugar, four eggs, two-thirds of a cupful of rich sour cream, a small teaspoonful of soda, half a nutmeg grated and four cupfuls of sifted flour. The cream should be the solid cream from the cream-pail, taken from the old fashioned milk-pan. If thin cream is used, a little more butter will be required. This makes one large or two small loaves, of excellent, satisfing cake that keeps nicely. Grandmother occasionally baked it in scolloped (sic) patty-pans.

DESSERTS

HOOVERIZED CANNED RASPBERRY CAKE
Successful Farming January, 1918

When America entered WWI in 1917, President Woodrow Wilson appointed Herbert Hoover as "Food Administrator." He was in charge of food production and conservation so that surpluses could be provided to American allies. "Food Will Win the War" became his motto as housewives were called upon to serve their families several meatless and wheatless meals each week.

Successful Farming magazine carried a monthly column called "The Way The Home Folks Helped Hoover," encouraging patriotic housewives to make War Bread (without white flour), War Pie (no top crust), and gave tips for making bread crumb cakes to use up every scrap of leftovers. In this recipe, brown sugar replaces scarce white sugar and fruit canned from the summer garden replaces commercially canned produce. You'd think the raspberries would just disappear with all the beating, but they sink to the bottom of this tasty pink cake. Serve it with vanilla ice cream.

½ cup butter	1½ cups flour
1 cup brown sugar	1 tsp. cinnamon
¼ cup buttermilk	1 tsp. soda
2 eggs	½ tsp. baking powder
1 tsp. lemon extract	¼ tsp. salt

1 cup canned raspberries and juice (you can substitute a thawed 12 oz. package of frozen berries and juice)

Cream the butter and sugar, and mix thoroughly. Sift together the dry ingredients. Add these, with the buttermilk, raspberries, eggs well beaten and lemon extract (or substitute lemon juice,) to the first mixture. Beat vigorously for two minutes. Pour into a loaf-cake pan which has been prepared with waxed paper. Bake 40 minutes in a moderately slow oven.

Author's Note: Pour into a buttered cake pan and bake about 25 minutes in a preheated 350° oven until top springs back and it's lightly browned. (If you use a loaf pan, bake at 325°.)

PICKLES

NEVER-FAIL DILL PICKLES
Food Fit for a King, Salem, W.Va., 1951

Start with fresh-picked small cucumbers for the best pickles. Keep these in unsealed jars in the refrigerator and they'll stay crisp. If you want to can pickles, choose a recipe with a higher percentage of vinegar. A pod of red pepper makes a nice addition to each jar.

20 pickling cucumbers	1 cup water
2 pieces dill	1 cup white vinegar
2 cloves garlic	1 Tbs. (kosher) salt

Pack 2 pint jars with well scrubbed, unpeeled cucumbers that have been sliced in half length-wise. Tuck a sprig of dill and a clove of garlic (split in half) in each jar. Now mix water, vinegar, and salt in a saucepan and bring to a boil. Pour hot liquid over cucumbers and refrigerate. Garlic fanciers will adore these.

Photo courtesy NC Archives and History

Pickle Etiquette
Any respectable chicken dinner calls for watermelon pickles or cucumber pickles. A ham or fresh pork dinner needs peach, or apple, or pear pickles to point it up. Chili sauce or a good sweet-sour pickle is preferred with beef and lamb. And for buffet dinners or supper parties, I like to put out an assortment of pickles as well as preserves.   Farm Journal *June, 1940*

PICKLES

PICKLED OKRA
Home Demonstration Club Cookbook, 1962

2 lbs. tender fresh okra
5 pods hot pepper
5 cloves peeled garlic
1 qt. white vinegar

½ cup water
6 Tbs. (kosher) salt
1 Tbs. celery seed

Wash okra and pack in 5 hot, sterilized pint jars. Put 1 pepper pod and 1 garlic clove in each jar. Bring remaining ingredients to boil. Pour over okra and seal. Let stand 8 weeks before using.

In a Cookbook From the Groom's Mother
Farm Journal & Farmer's Wife May, 1940

My Darling, here's a little book,
That tells you how I bake,
The cakes and pies and other good things,
His "mother used to make."
For men are hungry creatures, Dear,
But this we know about them,
That cooking would not be such fun,
If we had to eat without them.
So take this book with my fondest love,
And a thought I now impart;
When you feed a husband, keep in mind,
His stomach's near his heart!

Pickle Emergency
The Country Gentleman February, 1902

*"**Pickle Crop Short:** The Western Pickle Packer's Association has been considering an advance in prices. It is declared that there might be a pickle famine before next summer, and one of the packers said he would not be surprised if the supply gave out entirely before the close of summer."*

JAM

BLUEBERRY JELLY AND RELISH
Rural New-Yorker July, 1927

A brilliant recipe using the juice for jelly and the pulp for a sweet marmalade relish. For a sure outcome, you could use commercially powdered pectin, following the package directions for jelly, then follow recipe below for the relish. Read both recipes before beginning.

Jelly:
Wash berries and drain them; put them on to heat in a double boiler and let them heat 20 minutes. Then, put them in a double cheesecloth bag and let drip without much pressing. To 1½ cups juice add two cups sugar. Cook on low heat, stir and skim, cooking 5 minutes. Try a little; if it coats a spoon, pour into small hot jelly glasses; cover with melted paraffin.

Relish:
Take blueberries from bag after dripping juice. For every two quarts of blueberries, before they were heated, allow one cup hot water. Heat this up with the berries, stirring well. To every pint of pulp, add juice of one lemon and one orange, two cups sugar, one cup chopped, seeded raisins. Cook slowly till quite thick. Take from fire, add ¼ bottle (or packaged) commercial pectin, stir two minutes, seal in hot jars.

A home without hens is not much better than a comfortable railroad station.　　　　*Rural New-Yorker* November, 1926

JAM

ANNA'S CARROT JAM
From a 1914 newspaper clipping.

Just the thing to make with your bumper carrot crop. Why not serve your guests carrot jam on toast along with your special tomato cookies ? (See page 43 for tomato cookie recipe.)

Photo Courtesy of the Library of Congress

Although this is composed of the humblest ingredients, it never fails to prove a pleasing innovation. Not only because it is really delicious, but for the reason that it is apt to provoke a guessing contest. Here is the recipe:

Boil the carrots till they are tender. Drain and mash them through a colander. For each pound of carrot pulp, allow one pound of sugar and the juice of one lemon. Boil slowly until the mixture jellies and then set away in glasses.

PLUM CONSERVE
Farm Journal and Farmer's Wife June, 1941

4 lbs. plums, cut	1 lemon, juice
2 oranges, ground	½ lb. walnuts
1 cup raisins	Sugar

Pit and cut plums into chunks. Remove seeds from oranges and grind (use thin skinned oranges or tangerines.) Add raisins and measure fruit pulp. Add ¾ cup sugar for each cup fruit. Bring to boil, stirring constantly, then cook rapidly until thick and clear. Remove from fire, add lemon juice and nuts. Pour into jelly jars.

FARM JOKES

Photo Courtesy of NC Archives and History

THESE CHANGING TIMES
The Furrow, 1938

A farmer's wife who had no great respect for men anyhow, was hurrying from churn to sink, from sink to shed and back to the kitchen stove when she was asked if she wanted to vote. "No, I certainly don't," said she. "I say that, if there's one little thing the menfolks can do alone, for goodness' sake, let 'em do it."

The young lady from Boston was explaining: "Take an egg," she said, "and make a perforation in the base and a corresponding one in the apex. Then apply the lips to the aperature and, by forcibly exhaling the breath, discharge the shell of its contents."
An old lady who was listening exclaimed: "It beats all how folks do things nowadays. When I was a gal, they made a hole in each end and blew."

The teacher sent a note home with the boy: "Your son, Charles, shows signs of astigmatism. Will you please investigate and take steps to correct it?"
The next morning, she received a note from the father who wrote: "I don't exactly understand what Charlie has done, but I've walloped him, and you can wallop him tomorrow. That ought to help some."

FARM JOKES

ACTUAL PUBLISHED LETTERS
Farm Journal & Farmer's Wife
June, 1940

Irish couple, 26, want steady housework. Wife A-1 cook, congenial, attractive; husband understands everything.

In her breach-of-promise suit, Miss Manton alleges that on June 10th her employer put his arms around her and tried to kiss her. June 20, he succeeded.

The neckline of this well-fitting slip may be pointed or square, and an edging of *lice* is very nice.

For sale, seven room house, three rooms with hardwood floors; complete with bath and built-in inconveniences.

A woman approached the post office window belligerently. "I've been expecting a package containing medicine for a week and haven't received it yet!"

"Yes, Madam," said the post office clerk. "Kindly fill in this form and state the nature of your complaint."

"Well, it's no business of yours," the woman snapped, "but if you really must know, it's rheumatism. I have it very bad across my shoulders."   *Farm Life* November, 1927

Johnnie was absent from school one afternoon. The next morning the teacher received the following excuse: "Dear teacher, please excuse Johnnie's absence yesterday afternoon. He got his feet wet coming home at noon, and he didn't have any others to put on."
Rural New-Yorker, 1927

JUST WONDERING

Rural American families of times gone-by had to look no further than their monthly agricultural magazine for advice on everything from curing poultry diseases to mending broken hearts. Here's some timeless advice for families from farm journals that were "devoted to the farm, orchard, garden, poultry, and household economy."

FARM JOURNAL, 1885

"Advice for young housewives who do not know enough and older ones who do not know too much."

Q: *Should children be required to study their lessons in the evenings at home?*

A: Better an hour more in school if mind and body can both be free when school is out.

Farm woman with cream separator.

ADVICE FOR THE NEW YEAR
Successful Farming January, 1918

- *We are apt to measure a year by what we get out of it. We should, rather, measure it by what we put into it.*

- *Move into the New Year as you would into a new house. Carry with you only what is attractive or useful and make a bonfire of the old rubbish . . . chiefly useless memories and regrets.*

- *If 1918 is not the best year of my life, whom, probably, can I blame?*

JUST WONDERING

SUCCESSFUL FARMING, 1918

Q: *If a girl goes regularly with a young man, and when attending a basket social someone else buys her basket, should the man who purchased her basket see her home, or should the man she is going with?*
A: It does not necessarily follow that a man takes a lady home simply because he has purchased her basket at a basket social. If someone has asked for the privilege of taking her to the party, this may of course, provide other means for her company home.

Q: *What shall a girl answer when a boy wants to take her to supper and she wants to accept?*
A: In reply, you may say, "Thank you. I would be glad to go."

Q: *Should one eat candy in a theatre, either during the play or between the acts?*
A: According to the strictest propriety, it is in poor taste to chew gum, or eat candy in public. With the American public, however, candy and the theatre have become so closely associated, that it is offered for sale in almost every theatre, and many boxes of it are sold and enjoyed during the intermissions.

Thanks for the Buggy Ride

Q: *When a young man calls to take a lady auto riding, should he get out to assist her into the car?*
A: The man should stop his engine, go to the door and ask for her, just as he would in calling to take her any place else.

JUST WONDERING

CHATS WITH FARM LIFE GIRLS, 1927

Q: *What is the age when true love occurs?*
A: It's just about whatever age you happen to be when you fall in love. Generally speaking, it's the age when one is able to distinguish love from infatuation.

Q: *When a man starts to leave after having been introduced to a girl and says, "I'm glad I met you, Miss X," what would the girl say? Is it correct to say "thank you?"*
A: It is quite correct to say "thank you." The girl need not say anything else, but she must say that at least.

NEW ENGLAND FARM LIFE, 1929

Q: *I am five feet two inches tall and fifteen years old. Am I too young to go with boys and too young to work out?*
A: In some states you are too young for certain kinds of work. You decide about the dates.

Q: *I am an aviatrix and torn between love and flying. Which should I give up?* -Wings
A: Why give up either? That isn't the modern woman's way. Your boyfriend is probably resigned to your flying. A man shouldn't propose to an aviatrix otherwise; she's too likely to take him up!

Q: *Should the mother of a young girl let the daughter choose her own dresses, hats, shoes? I don't like the things she wishes to buy for me and she doesn't like the things I choose for myself.* –Sixteen
A: I think most mothers and daughters have to compromise on that score. You want clothes that reflect your own personality, but mothers usually have ideas worth considering.

JUST WONDERING

FARM JOURNAL AND FARMER'S WIFE, 1941

Dear Polly;
Q: *How can I slip out with my boyfriend without my family knowing about it?*
A: And what's so awfully wrong with their knowing about it? They may tease you a little bit, but you can take it. Of course, if it's because you think your parents will object, that's different. Talk it over with your mother sometime when you and she are doing the dishes. And then do as agreed.

Dear Polly;
Q: *Are there any boys who don't park and pet? It almost seems as though there aren't. And if a girl objects, it seems as though the boys don't bother with her afterwards. What can be done?*
A: From the letters I've had from boys, I'd say that there are a good many who don't park and pet. They want to respect their girls. Look around you, and you'll find some.

Dear Polly;
Q: *My mother will not let me wear anklets or volleyball suits. How can I get her to let me?*
A: Gym suits or shorts are NOT for street wear; though anklets are acceptable for casual school dress, as well as for sports. Surely you can strike up a compromise with your mother so that you may wear sox and shorts for active sports.

Photo Courtesy of the NC Archives and History

REMEDIES

SOME MARVELOUS REMEDIES
Hearth & Home 1905-1906

If any sister knows of a plain home re-medy for Torpid Liver, I shall be very thankful to receive it.   -Mrs. A. Cromley

Sick of tobacco? New remedy sent free to be given secretly in tea, coffee, and food. Oh! The joy as your man or boy rejoices to be free from bondage.

If you suffer from Falling Sickness, send for a free bottle of Epilepticide and test it.

Wonderful life-giving doctor. Cures cancer, consumption, and all bacterial diseases.

Try Professor Jules LaBorde's marvelous French preparation of Calthus for Lost Manhood.

You know this famous bottle~Keep it handy~ Good for humans, too

Everybody wants a gold tooth. Gold teeth, the latest fad. Fill your own teeth. A gold plated shell that fits any tooth. Looks like regular dentist's work. Fools them all. 10 cents each. 4 for 25 cents.

Too fat? Take off double chin, big stomach, fat hips. No starving.

Never stand afar and view with fear and trembling that which lies in your way. Face it boldly and see how very small it is, after all.
Hearth & Home, 1905

Just keep on smiling cheerfully, if hope is nearly gone.
And bristle up and grit your teeth, and keep on keepin' on.
Farm Life, 1927

HOUSEHOLD HINTS

HOW TO CATCH FIRE?
Farm Journal March, 1885

- To protect the feet from the cold when riding, put a lighted lantern under the robe.
- A few grains of red pepper sprinkled in the soles of the stockings will keep warm the coldest pair of feet.

Farm Journal August, 1882

How about that drain from the kitchen sink? Clean it out or it will breed typhoid fever.

Farm Journal March, 1885

Non-essentials should be indulged in sparingly by farmers' wives. It is better to be a jolly, healthy, practically useful woman, than to be a puny, fashionable nonentity. Women should always bear in mind that their first duty is to themselves.

EVERY FARM WIFE NEEDS . . .
Farm Life September, 1927

- Several neat, becoming, washable house dresses.
- At least two pairs of well-fitting, low-heeled work shoes.
- A substantial cook stove, with a reliable oven.
- A kitchen sink, with running water and ample supply of hot water from the range reservoir.
- An icebox, if ice is available, or a handy cellar with steps that don't threaten to break the farm wife's neck or back.
- A washing machine if the power is available, or tub; a wringer, unchipped washboards, trustworthy clothes lines, and a comfortable place to wash outside the kitchen.
- An electric iron, if she can get power, otherwise a gasoline iron.

1930's gasoline iron

LAUNDRY

GONNA SOAP MY BLUES AWAY
by Kathryn Williams
Farm Journal & Farmer's Wife January, 1940

Thank God tomorrow's Monday,
And I have to wash the clothes;
I can think of soap and bluing
And forget about my woes,
I can scrub away my heartaches
Turn my troubles inside out
Run my worries through the wringer,
Let the wind iron out my doubt.
I can starch my weak excuses
Scrub away my flimsy fears,
Build a palisade on clothes lines
And shut out all worldly jeers.

Photo Courtesy of Mars Hill College

CREDITS

VINTAGE AGRICULTURAL JOURNALS

Successful Farming
Farmer's Wife
Farm Journal
Farm Journal & Farmer's Wife
New England Farm Life
The Furrow
Poultry Tribune

Country Gentleman
Farm & Fireside
Farm Home
Farm Life
The Rural New-Yorker
The Progressive Farmer

BOOKS

Atkeson, Mary Meek, *The Woman on the Farm*, 1924
Dishes Men Like, 1952
Home Demonstration Club of Asheville, NC Cookbook, 1951
Home Demonstration Club of Mecklenburg County, NC, 1962
Home Demonstration Club of Salem, WVa Cookbook, 1950
Home Comfort Wood Cookstove Cook Book, 1933
Iced Dainties, 1928
Majestic Range Wood Cookstove Cook Book, 1890

RESOURCES FOR COOKING WITH WOOD

Woodstove Cookery: At Home on the Range, by Jane Cooper, 1977
Lehman's Non-Electric Catalog: www.lehmans.com (888) 438-5346
    The fabulous catalog costs $4.00.
Vintage wood cookstove cookbooks by early stove manufacturers can be purchased at antique stores and online auctions.

THANKS!

To Effie Price, my favorite "farm wife." Steve Millard, cover design, the crack research team of Kathy McGuigan, Marti Otto, and Richard Renfro. Taste testers included David Currier, McLean Bissell, Lora Pendleton, Sara Webb, Annie, Wes, Rita, and Wayne Erbsen (all are still alive.) Proofreaders Janet Swell, David Currier, Bonnie Neustein, Beverly Teeman, Biltmore Press, and recipe editor, Jennifer Thomas. Thanks to my husband and publisher, Wayne *"dishes-that-farm-men-like"* Erbsen, for support and pestering me to finish this book.

RECIPE INDEX

NATIVE GROUND MUSIC

BOOKS OF SONGS & LORE
Backpocket Bluegrass Songbook
Backpocket Old-Time Songbook
Cowboy Songs, Jokes & Lingo
Front Porch Songs & Stories
Old-Time Gospel Songbook
Outlaw Ballads, Legends, & Lore
Railroad Fever
Rousing Songs of the Civil War
Log Cabin Pioneers
Rural Roots of Bluegrass

INSTRUCTION BOOKS
5-String Banjo for the
    Complete Ignoramus!
Bluegrass Banjo Simplified!!
Painless Guide to the Guitar
Painless Mandolin Melodies
Southern Mountain Banjo
Southern Mountain Fiddle
Southern Mountain Guitar
Southern Mountain Mandolin
Southern Mountain Dulcimer

RECORDINGS
Authentic Outlaw Ballads
Ballads & Songs of the Civil War
Bullfrogs on Your Mind
Cowboy Songs
Front Porch Favorites
Love Songs of the Civil War
The Home Front
Log Cabin Songs

Old-Time Gospel Favorites
Raccoon and a Possum
Railroadin' Classics
Railroad Fever
Singing Rails
Songs of the Santa Fe Trail
Southern Mountain Classics
Southern Soldier Boy

MORE HISTORIC COOKBOOKS BY BARBARA SWELL
Log Cabin Cooking
Take Two and Butter 'Em While They're Hot!
Children at the Hearth
Secrets of the Great Old-Timey Cooks
Mama's in the Kitchen

Write or call for a FREE Catalog:
Native Ground Music
109 Bell Road
Asheville, NC 28805
(800) 752-2656
Web Site: **www.nativeground.com**
Email: **banjo@nativeground.com**